DSC SPEED READS

MANAGEMENT

CW00499474

Team Building

Brian Rothwell

DIRECTORY OF SOCIAL CHANGE

Published by
Directory of Social Change
24 Stephenson Way
London NW1 2DP
Tel. 08450 77 77 07; Fax 020 7391 4804
email publications@dsc.org.uk
www.dsc.org.uk
from whom further copies and a full books catalogue are available.

Directory of Social Change is a Registered Charity no. 800517

First published 2009

ISBN 978 1 906294 18 2

British Library Cataloguing in Publication Data

A catalogue record for this book is available from the British Library

Cover and text designed by Kate Bass
Typeset by Marlinzo Services, Frome
Printed and bound by Martins of Berwick

All Directory of Social Change departments in London:
08450 77 77 07

Directory of Social Change Northern Office:
Research 0151 708 0136

Contents

Introduction

Who will this book help?

This practical guide will help all managers who are responsible for the performance of others. In particular it will aid individuals who are new to management, and it will add value to managers who are unused to building a team and those who recognise that they have a problem with the concept.

Building a team is not an easy task because teams are often inherited groups of people that have not been chosen with 'teamness' in mind. Individuals may have been selected for the technical skills that they can add to the team equation rather than their role as supportive team members. Team building requires effort and perseverance, often in the face of discouragement and disappointment. It does not work all of the time. Ask any elite coach of a sports team activity and they will tell you that this sense of teamness is an elusive goal that is rarely achieved.

What will it give you?

This book provides guidance on how to make sure that team building works well and, as a consequence, should help to bring about greater managerial satisfaction. Adhering to these guidelines will enable you to get a job done more efficiently and to develop members of staff as team players.

Chapter 1

What is a team?

This chapter defines a team and looks at what makes a team great. It looks at the three qualities that a successful team should possess, and how to achieve this.

A team is a group of people who are working together for a common purpose. Boards of directors need to work together as a team. So do senior managers, departmental members, project groups, customer support teams and volunteers. The issues involved in building a team remain the same, irrespective of seniority.

A team differs from a professional association in that the team members have a sense of direction, belonging and identity. The members use these three senses to produce results that are not only quantitative and can be measured, but also qualitative: in terms that indicate how the team members feel about their jobs and colleagues.

A sense of direction

A sense of team direction comes from:

- a team vision
- team members knowing they have to play to each other's strengths and compensate for each other's weaknesses, in order to bring the vision into reality.

5

A group of people cannot become a team without a vision or goal in which all the members believe. A vision provides individuals with the hope that the future will be better than the present. However, it is more than that. Having a clear idea of how things could be, and the direction in which the team is heading, enables everyone to make the day-to-day small decisions to move towards the big picture.

All the members cannot be outstanding performers at every task that the team is required to perform. Some are better at certain tasks than others and vice versa. Good teamwork involves playing to each individual's strengths and compensating for their weaknesses by helping them out as necessary. This only happens when everyone is working as a team.

A sense of identity

A sense of identity is brought about when the team:

- shares the same set of values
- has a set of agreed behavioural rules
- produces outstanding results by taking risks together.

Values are the deeply-held beliefs that guide our actions or make us feel uneasy or guilty on occasions. If one of our values is honesty, we may feel guilty at telling a little white lie, even if our motives are good. Being clear about what team values are makes it easier to get along together and makes team decision making so much easier. In order for a team to aspire to greatness, it is important that it shares the same set of values.

Teams also need to know how to behave, both when they are together and apart. Without such a set of rules, team greatness cannot be achieved.

Top tip

Create guidelines:

'Our *Black Book of Teamship Rules* is fundamental to coaching... I wouldn't even run a business without one now.'

Sir Clive Woodward, elite sports coach

A sense of belonging

A sense of belonging in a team is derived from:

- individual self-confidence and being confident about the abilities of teammates
- trusting each other
- having fun together.

The individual needs of members always vary. A high-performing team will create a climate where individuals are valued for themselves and not just for the knowledge and skills that they bring. In such a team, each member has confidence in themselves and the others to do what is right to achieve the agreed goals.

This comes about only by building trust between team members. Trust in another individual exists in an imaginary bank account that resides inside all of our heads. We all trust some individuals more than others. People can make deposits in this trust account by the actions that they take, and they can make withdrawals by taking other actions that destroy trust. These accounts can be in the black or in the red. In a great team, all of these trust accounts are healthily in the black.

The openness, support and trust that is provided by a highly performing team will always enable people to become aware of their own individuality, recognise their self-worth and raise their self-confidence.

If you ask people whether they enjoy working in their assigned team, this remark is almost always among the positive responses:

> *'I like the people – they are fun to be with. We have a laugh together.'*

Members of successful teams enjoy being with each other. Enjoyment comes not only from success but also

Case study

Mike Walker, a banker, describes the only good boss he ever worked for in 1990:
'He's open and honest with us, treats everyone fairly, does what he says he is going to do and he admits it when he's made a mistake. He gives praise and recognition when it's deserved but doesn't overdo it. He tells you squarely when he thinks you're not pulling your weight. I've never seen him make a withdrawal from the account by doing something that would cause me to trust him less.'

from comradeship, and this arises from having fun and laughing together.

The characteristics of a great team

Great teams have nine characteristics. They consist of individuals who:

Where next?

The Last Word on Power, T Goss, Bantam, 1995.
Winning, C Woodward, Hodder & Stoughton, 2004.

1 have an agreed vision
2 complement each others' strengths and compensate for each others' weaknesses
3 believe in a shared set of values
4 understand the rules of how to behave in team situations and when apart
5 produce outstanding results
6 take risks together by attempting to do what may seem to be impossible in pursuit of the goal
7 are confident in their own abilities and have confidence that their teammates will make the right contribution
8 trust one another completely
9 have fun together.

It is the job of the team leader to establish a sense of direction, a sense of identity and a sense of belonging. However, once this has been achieved, in great teams the accountability is both mutual and shared. Individuals in such teams say: 'We hold ourselves accountable for the whole team performance', rather than 'The boss holds each of us accountable for our own results'.

These nine characteristics apply irrespective of whether the team is based in one room or scattered across the world.

Chapter 2

Setting the team goalposts

This chapter defines a team vision and looks at how to create one. A team vision is an ambitious dream about where the team could go and what it could achieve.

Vision statements

A vision statement should be:

- communicable
- memorable
- achievable
- sustainable
- inspirational.

It need not be measurable. It can be likened to a:

- **compass** – in that it gives a team a clear direction
- **dynamo** – in that it generates energy and enthusiasm
- **sounding board** – in that it resonates with the values and aspirations of all in the team
- **beacon** – in that it shines to show the team the way to go.

Here is a good example:

> *'We are ladies and gentlemen serving ladies and gentlemen.'*
> Staff vision statement, Europa Hotel, Belfast

Top tip

Ensure that all team plans, strategic or operational, and all financial budgets lead towards the vision. If they do not, revise the plans and the budgets.

Edgar Parnell, former Director, The Plunkett Foundation

A vision statement embraces more than the literal words that it contains. To those involved, the vision can mean many things, and these things are what the team members decide. The example vision statement embraces standards of courtesy, service and timeliness that customers often find uncommon in the hotel trade. It also provides a way to determine how the hotel members of staff should behave towards each other.

It is a common misconception that a vision can be constructed only from the top of an organisation. This is not true – all teams need their own vision. If your organisation has a vision and it is a good one, you may like to link the vision of your area of operations to it. If it is a mediocre one, you may wish to ignore it when creating a vision for your own department. If your organisation does not have a vision, please do not use this as an excuse not to formulate one for your people.

Top tip

Make sure that every member of your team has a copy of the vision. Display a poster version on the wall to help the team remember it, and so that they can refer to it at any time.

Heather Brierley, Training Consultant, DSC

Creating a vision statement

Dos and don'ts

Don't confuse a vision with an intention – a vision should not start with the word 'To'.

Don't fudge by using words such as 'best' – they endanger credibility and seldom inspire.

Don't use jargon, it will not mean anything to those outside the organisation.

Don't try to compromise by combining unrelated themes.

Don't impose your vision on other team members.

Don't think that a vision will be a substitute for proper operational planning.

Where next?

It's Tough at the Top, D Allcock Tyler, DSC, 2006. See chapter 3: 'No vision, no insight'.

Do brainstorm the ingredients of the vision with your team – these are best expressed in single words, rather than phrases or sentences.

Do create the vision in the present tense, so as to reinforce the sense of 'being in the midst of it'.

Do be prepared to suspend your own preconceptions.

Do test the vision – 'What, if anything, has X which we currently involved in (or Y that we are now pursuing) got to do with our vision?'

Do give the vision time to mature – first versions nearly always can be improved.

Experiencing the team vision

Ask the team members to describe what they see and feel when contemplating the vision. For example:

See:	Feel:
▪ delighted customers	▪ pride
▪ fulfilled colleagues	▪ energy
▪ harmony among stakeholders	▪ wider sense of purpose
▪ strong demand for products	▪ achievement
▪ potential volunteers eager to join.	▪ happiness in being part of the organisation.

The team leader needs to encourage team members to refer consistently to the vision and the direction in which the team is going. This helps to reinforce belief in the vision. It needs to be done in one-to-one situations, small groups, large presentations and all dealings with the media. The team leader also needs to take responsibility for challenging activities that are already underway, perhaps due to history, which do not contribute to delivery of the vision.

Top tip

Experiment with imagery – 'Give them cathedrals to build' (Voltaire), or 'Land of milk and honey' (Moses).

Debra Allcock Tyler, Chief Executive, DSC

Where next?

Leadership for Dummies, M Loeb; S Kindle, IDG Books Worldwide, 1999. *Reinventing Co-operation,* E Parnell, The Plunkett Foundation, 2001.

Chapter 3

Shared values

This chapter defines a set of values, describes the process of creating a shared set of team values and illustrates how to use them.

Creating a set of team values

We looked at values in chapter 1, and found that they are the deeply-held beliefs that guide our actions. A set of values is a list of four or five words or short phrases that guide our behaviours, in that they help us to decide what is right or wrong. Again, being clear about what our team values are makes it easier to get along and makes decision-making much simpler.

Steps to define values

Bring the team together and allocate a time of about two hours. Make sure that there are writing materials for everyone and that there is a flipchart and plenty of sticky notes available.

Explain that the objective is to define the team's set of shared values, which will help to achieve the agreed vision.

Procedure to define values

Ask each of them to think of two or three of their close friends and note down the personal qualities that make them attractive: for example, a sense of humour or always being willing to listen (point 1).

Ask them what each friend would have to do to end the friendship, for example, perhaps by making fun of them or their family, or breaking a confidence about something personal that they have told them. Ask them to note these down beside the qualities they have already recorded (point 2).

Then ask them to think of one or two people whom they dislike or who irritate them. Request that they each note down the main reason for this: for example, perhaps one doesn't do what they promise to, and the other gossips behind everyone's back (point 3).

Now ask them what each of these individuals actually do that could possibly make them overlook the fault that they have noted: for example, perhaps by always looking on the positive side of things, or in the case of a colleague, being good with difficult customers – whatever it is that makes them think that the person is not so bad after all (point 4).

Tell them that process points 1 and 4 should suggest similar values: in the examples above they could be a positive attitude and or a willingness to listen.

In the same way, process points 2 and 3 should suggest similar things but in a negative way. Being unreliable and untrustworthy might be the common themes. Ask them to turn these into positive values so that, for example, they become reliability and trustworthiness. Next, ask them to pool their results on a flipchart.

Issue each team member with three sticky notes and ask them to label them 1, 2 and 3. Then invite them to come forward to the flipchart and place the label with a 3 on it next to the value that they think is most important, a 2 next to the value that they decide is the second most important, and the 1 against the value that they think is least important. Then add up the scores against each potential value to reveal the result.

Where next?

Core Coaching: Coaching for Great Performance at Work, S Maguire, DSC, 2008. See the section on coaching teams.

13

In this way you should reach a shortlist of four or five values that are thought to be the most important to the team. They should reveal the fundamental attitudes that define the team and will guide how they act and why. A list of potential values which have been used in organisations is shown below – it is not meant to be definitive, merely descriptive.

Achievement	Expertise	Optimism
Adventure	Freedom	Patience
Assertiveness	Generosity	Personal development
Challenge	Growth	Quality
Change	Helping others	Reputation
Competence	Honesty	Recognition
Confidence	Humility	Relationships
Commitment	Humour	Resilience
Cooperation	Integrity	Responsibility
Courage	Independence	Security
Creativity	Influence	Self-esteem
Decisiveness	Involvement	Self-reliance
Discretion	Joyfulness	Self-respect
Dynamism	Justice	Stability
Effectiveness	Knowledge	Subtlety
Encouragement	Loyalty	Truth
Equality	Merit	Trust
Ethics	Objectivity	Wealth
Excellence	Openness	Wisdom

Using team values

Suppose that the set of five team values that you have created is as follows:

- honesty
- courage
- wisdom
- justice
- humility.

Now, suppose that you have a big team decision to make that will affect other people. It may be to:

- close a branch of the operation
- choose a new computer supplier
- make 20 staff redundant
- do business with an organisation whose values you suspect
- move the administration function out of London.

You can now test the decision you have made against your values by asking your team members the following questions.

- Is this an honest decision?
- Is this a courageous decision?
- Is this a wise decision?
- Is this a just decision?
- Is this a humble decision?

Sometimes it is useful to get every individual to score the decision against each value on a scale of 1 to 10, with 10 perfectly meeting the value and 1 failing to meet the value at all. The results are then pooled. If the answer to any of the above reflects a low score, the decision is not true to the team's values and should be reconsidered.

Where next?

Committed Enterprise: How to Make Values and Visions Work,
H Davidson, Butterworth-Heinemann, 2002.

Chapter 4

Agreeing behavioural rules

This chapter shows an example of behavioural rules: a set of rules put together by the board of directors of a small to medium-sized farming cooperative to govern their conduct when together and apart.

As mentioned in Chapter 1, all members of great teams know how to behave when together and apart. Sometimes these behavioural rules emerge informally over time, but usually it is best to commit them to paper, as then they can be referred to as guidelines. Acceptance of the rules is greatly enhanced if all team members contribute to their creation.

The example below involves a team of board directors. However, the rules shown can be adapted to any team, irrespective of their level of seniority.

Behavioural rules for board directors

Induction

1. We have a formal induction programme that all directors are required to undertake.

Attendance

2. Directors are expected to attend all board meetings.

3. Meeting dates will be set annually in September for the following calendar year.

4. Any emergency board meetings will be scheduled with as much notice as possible.

Board papers

5. Board papers and an agenda will be sent to directors seven days before a board meeting.

6. Individual directors are expected to ask questions of the relevant person on any topic that that they do not understand before the meeting.

7. Board members are expected to devote sufficient time to ensuring that they fully understand all of the material that they are sent.

8. Board discussions are limited to those issues upon which we have all received paperwork. No unexpected issues are introduced at our meetings.

Minutes

9. Minutes will be issued by the secretary within 48 hours of the end of a meeting.

10. Minutes record decisions taken and the reasons why. They also report who has agreed to do what, by when and to what standard. They do not record what was said at meetings.

11. When individual directors have agreed to take action on behalf of the board, they are expected to act with integrity and complete the action to the time and standard required.

Top tip

When there is no clear individual who is responsible for writing minutes rotate the task – it makes everyone feel involved and builds skills.

Heather Brierley, Training Consultant, DSC

12. If they are not able to complete the action, early notice to the chairperson is expected.

Decision making

13. Decisions are made by consensus.

14. We consider the needs of all stakeholders when making a decision.

15. When a decision is reached, the chairperson will ask for that decision to be minuted.

16. After a decision is taken, board members are expected to demonstrate full support for the decision.

Personal demeanour at board meetings

17. Directors are expected to dress smartly at all times when representing the organisation.

18. Board members are expected to arrive 15 minutes early for board meetings.

19. Our meetings start on time and every effort will be made to finish on time.

20. We attempt to follow the agenda at all times.

21. All remarks at board are made through the chairperson.

22. We all allow our colleagues to finish what they are saying without interruption.

23. We address the chairperson as 'Chair' and our board colleagues by their christian name.

24. Everybody is regarded as equal in board meetings.

25. The chairperson controls the boardroom process, not the subject matter discussed.

Top tip

Suggest a good-humoured penalty system for late attendance at meetings. At DSC senior management team meetings, any culprits put one pound in the pot for each minute they are late. The aim is to encourage timeliness in a fun way, and any money collected goes to a nominated charity.

Debra Allcock Tyler, Chief Executive, DSC

26. Our board meetings encourage objective debate, but not personal debate. We strive to separate the person from the issue under discussion.

27. We regard listening as more important than speaking at meetings.

28. Silence from a director is to be regarded as assent.

29. All opinions are respected at our board meetings.

30. Appropriate humour is encouraged.

Out-of-meeting communications

31. Directors are encouraged to communicate outside meetings by face-to-face, one-to-one informal meetings, phone and email.

32. It is expected that every director has an email address and refers to their email daily.

33. Phone calls between directors are encouraged, but not at anti-social hours.

Director appraisal

34. Once a year, part of a board meeting is devoted to an appraisal of the performance of all directors on the board, including the chairperson.

35. Where training needs are identified, directors are required to devote time and energy to ensure that the necessary learning is carried out.

36. Where expense is involved with director training, the organisation will pay subject to approval from the finance director.

Personal responsibilities of directors

37. We seek to promote and advance the status, profile and reputation of the organisation at all times.

Top tip

Get your team around a table with pens and a flip chart paper. Ask them, with you, to note down any behavioural rules they think are important for the team. Once on paper, you can create a polished list to which everyone feels committed and can refer to as guiding principles.

38. We are professional in all of our dealings.

39. The organisation as a whole is more important than any one part.

40. Directors are expected to put the organisation before any personal self-interest.

41. We do not use our position as directors for personal gain.

42. What is said at meetings is regarded as confidential and must not be divulged to outside persons.

43. As directors we make responsible use of the resources of the organisation.

44. We are responsible for the modesty of the expenses that we incur on the organisation's behalf.

The set of rules above not only binds the behaviour of the current directors but it also serves as an induction tool for any new members of the board, and therefore makes integration into the team much easier. The rules are formally reviewed once a year as a formal item on the board's agenda.

Where next?

Codes of Conduct for Trustees, C Farmer, Charity Trustee Networks, 2008.

Chapter 5

Handling strengths and weaknesses

This chapter delineates a process for identifying individual strengths within a team and for compensating for individual weaknesses. It provides a technique, the Hot Chair process, to help achieve this.

A team can be built only by spending time together face to face. There is no substitute for this. Even remote teams spread around the world need to meet on a regular basis if they are to become a team. The trick is to ensure that the time spent is focused not only on the tasks in hand, but also on team-building activities.

One of the best such exercises identifies the perceived strengths and weaknesses of each individual team member. It is called the 'Hot Chair Process'. It can be used in many different ways and at different times, but it is particularly useful in identifying the behaviours that are needed from all members of the team in order to bring a vision into being. It should take less than an hour in a team of six people.

The Hot Chair process

Arrange the furniture so that there is a chair for every team member in a circle, with one for you as the leader in the centre. It helps if there are no barriers such as desks or training room tables behind which individuals can hide their body language.

Arrange for blank flipchart sheets to be posted around the room. Write up the agreed vision for the team on one of them so that it reminds everyone present of the future goal.

Where next?

The Pleasure and the Pain: the No-fibbing Guide to Working with People, D Allcock Tyler, DSC, 2007.

Ensure that there are writing materials in front of everyone. Explain the following process and state that you as the leader will go first to give an example. Emphasise that you want openness and honesty from everyone and that the objective is to move from the vision to actionable behaviours.

Explain that each member of the team is to spend some time in silence, thinking about how you, as the team leader, can be of more assistance to each person in helping to achieve the agreed vision. Say that you would like them all to write down:

- one thing they want more of from you
- one thing they want less of from you
- one thing that you could do together as a pair or as a subset of the team.

When everyone has indicated that they are ready, tell them that you will go around the circle, and then everyone will say what they have written down. State that you will write down what everyone has said without any comment, unless you are unclear as to what is being said. At the end of this part of the process, you should have written down three points from each team member, and every one of them should help the team to go forward together.

Then explain that it will be someone else's turn to sit in the middle, in the 'Hot Chair', and the process will be repeated. Keep doing that until everyone has had a turn.

When everyone has finished, take some quiet time for team members to think through what their colleagues have said about them. Ask them each to commit to what they are going to do, and by when, to help each other and the team as a whole to go forward towards the vision. Allocate a blank flipchart sheet to each individual so that they can record what they are committing to do. In this way, everyone will be able to see what all of their teammates are promising.

At the end of the process, each person's flipchart should look something like this:

I promise more:	I promise less:	I promise together:
team building activities	last minute requests	Donna and I will visit a prospective donor
briefings on how the pipeline will affect team members	of my time will be spent behind the computer screen	Ted and I will review our finance processes
attendance at team meetings	working late in the office	Kim and I will meet to discuss the six-month schedule

Where next?

Leadership 101, M Lloyd; B Rothwell, DSC, 2007.

If conducted properly, this exercise allows each member to:

■ identify their strengths and weaknesses, as perceived by their colleagues

■ make requests for help and assistance in the interests of teamwork

■ commit to help each other for the benefit of the team as a whole.

Chapter 6

Risk, confidence and trust

This chapter looks at how teams can produce outstanding results by being willing to try something new, and introduces the key to team building: developing the self-esteem of all team members. It also examines the issue of trust.

Case study

Ann Paul, formerly record-breaking fundraising director for RNIB was willing to take a risk. She said to her team: *'Let's see if we can hold the annual fundraising dinner at Buckingham Palace and have Rod Stewart singing live as our guests walk in. Are we all in agreement?'*

High-performing teams not only produce outstanding quantifiable results, they also take risks together to achieve their goals. They are prepared to try what has not been tried before.

Taking risks and identifying possibilities

Great team leaders neither believe that they are paid a salary for what is there already, nor do they believe they are paid for what is going to happen anyway. They think they are paid to identify the possibility that currently, something is missing, and when they have identified what is lacking, it is their responsibility to invent something to fill the gap. What they do is to drive their teams towards these twin objectives.

Case study

An educational establishment catering for 16–19 year-olds suffered a severe cut in its funding from the local government. Its transformation was to establish a driving school. It did this because many young adults learn to drive, and driving lessons could be made part of the curriculum easily. Parents were delighted to be able to pay for their children to be taught as part of the school day. In its first year, this experiment more than made up for the deficit in funding and the programme still exists.

Exploring possibilities

The trick is for teams to be willing to enter into conversations about possibilities that may improve the current situation. There are many kinds of conversations for possibility – some are structured, and some are informal. Conversations of this type are the primary source of creativity, ideas and innovation.

Managing the discussion

In order to be meaningful, a conversation about possibilities must be about a project that currently looks impossible but is not an illusion, rather a heartfelt desire. While they are very natural, conversations for possibility virtually never occur naturally. They do not happen in ordinary day-to-day discussions or meetings, but have to be managed. The following are tips for managing such a conversation.

People need to know that this is a conversation for possibility. They need to know that it is safe to speculate and propose ideas. It is also useful to tell them how long the conversation will last.

Top tip

Don't limit your thinking: there is nothing threatening about a possibility.

25

No evaluation of ideas takes place until all of the ideas are presented – potential missiles have to be kept in their firing tubes during this part of the conversation.

No decisions are made – individuals are not committing themselves to anything by either speaking or listening during the conversation.

Conversations for possibility honour the past without being bound by it. There is no guarantee that the future has to be a mere extension of the past. Our experience is limited to the past, but our imagination is not. We can stand in the future and look backwards, and we can invent the future *from* the future, if we so desire.

'What if?' and 'How about?' are useful ways to offer a new idea or challenge a limiting point of view. For example: 'What would the possibility look like if we could overcome this problem?' 'How about looking at his problem from a different angle?'

After the 'ideas' stage comes the 'evaluation' stage. This is when we have to categorise the ideas generated. Some will be worth taking forward, others need to be shelved and thought about, and others further still will need putting in the bin.

There will come a time when a stand will need to be taken on one idea, on one possibility, in order to convert it into an opportunity by agreeing to take some kind of action.

Where next?

The Art of Possibility, B Zander, Penguin, 2000.

Building confidence

High-performing teams demonstrate their belief in each other all the time. The job of the team leader is to start off this process and encourage everyone else to do the same. This is shown in the following table.

Building relationships	■ Getting to know people as individuals and understanding their hopes and aspirations ■ Listening to people ■ Being generous in sharing knowledge, skills and expertise
Being clear and enthusiastic	■ Demonstrating a belief in the team vision by living as though it already exists ■ Translating the vision into a mission and then into goals with strategies and milestones ■ Agreeing targets and parameters with individuals and the team as a whole ■ Putting requests across with enthusiasm and conviction
Being honest and encouraging others to do so	■ Acting with sincerity, openness and fairness to all ■ Celebrating successes with the team and individuals ■ Giving accurate and timely feedback, both good and bad ■ Demonstrating that you are prepared to 'fight your corner' for the team ■ Acknowledging difficulties and involving others in finding solutions
Building ownership among team members	■ Permitting easy access to as much information as possible ■ Delegating as much as you can and ensuring that individuals have the authority to make the necessary decisions ■ Asking for others' opinions and listening to their responses ■ Allowing people the time to resolve their own problems ■ Promoting wide-ranging development opportunities ■ Acting as coach to team members whenever possible

Top tip

An effective and inexpensive way to recognise and motivate a team member when they have done well is to send them a homemade postcard listing one of your team values. On the postcard write a note of praise about how they have fulfilled that value.

**Ellie Vaughan,
Reward and
Recognition
Advisor, Cancer
Research UK**

Where next?

How to Win Friends and Influence People, D Carnegie, Ebury Press, 1998.

Importance of praise in building self-esteem

Psychologists know that healthy humans, both adults and children, need praise in order to develop and grow in confidence. Recently there have been reports of research in America which suggest that people at work receive five times less praise than they need.

Think of the last time someone said 'Well done!' to you. If it was someone whose judgement you respected, you probably felt good about the task and yourself as a result. Merited praise builds self-esteem. The best praise is from one person to another, face-to-face. A close second is a handwritten note (not an email). It can be given either privately or in public.

Praising team members

Dos and don'ts

Do mean it.

Do be alert to opportunities to give praise whenever and wherever it is deserved – you will not make it meaningless by doing it often.

Do give the praise as soon as it is deserved, rather than saving it for later.

Do praise small successes as well as large ones.

Do praise as many people as possible.

Do pass on praise from elsewhere and let the person know that their work has been noticed: for example, 'The MD and several board members have told me how good it was.'

Don't use praise in order to flatter or as a means of trying to get someone to work.

Don't praise actions which have called for no particular effort.

Don't debase praise by using it randomly or thoughtlessly.

Trusting one another

Trust cannot be gained by demand. 'You'll just have to trust me on this' is often a weak excuse by a manager or team member who either does not know the answer, or is unwilling to share the necessary information with the team. In either case the statement is most likely to have the opposite of the intended effect – to make the listeners more sceptical rather than more trusting.

The extent to which trust is maintained and grows is dependent on how the team leader behaves all the time. The analogy of trust as a bank account presented in Chapter 1 is relevant here – there are no exceptions to this truism.

Some people are willing to trust others from the outset, expecting the best. These people can be a real support and source of quick feedback. They tend to have deeply-held beliefs and convictions and, if someone does or says something that loses their trust, they can become extremely critical, taking a very long time to begin to trust again.

Where next? *W* *N E S*

The One Minute Manager, K Blanchard; S Johnson, HarperCollins, 2004.

Case study

Paul Own, a board member, said this during an appraisal process:
> *'I'll tell you why I trust you. It's because you enjoy fun and laughter. Because you have a sense of proportion and a sense of the ridiculous … you don't take it personally when I say "No" to you.*
>
> *You take my advice and think about it. You do what you say you are going to do. We believe in the same things, we share the values we put together. You treat me as an equal [and] put my needs before your own.*
>
> *You don't mind admitting your mistakes and laughing about them. You stand up for yourself and for me. You're growing as a person and like to learn new things, and fundamentally have a good opinion of yourself.'*

At the other extreme are those who are sceptical of the trustworthiness of others from the outset. Generally they can be won over gradually, once they have satisfied themselves, based on their own experience that they are unlikely to be let down. Any setback will result in almost irreparable harm to the relationship.

Where next?

Serving to Lead, B Rothwell, Authorhouse, 2008.

The difficulty is that we all use different trust currencies, and unless team members are using the correct currency, there is no deposit. Some individuals feel trusted when they are given a free rein and have their ideas respected. Others feel trusted when their feelings and the feelings and reactions of others are taken into account. Others further still feel trusted when they have clear goals and are rewarded for achieving them. Finally, some feel trusted when they are consulted and see things happen according to the agreed rules. Team leaders and members need to know their people, respect their differences and react accordingly to build trust.

Chapter 7

Having fun

Life and work should be fun, and relationships within teams should be too. This chapter looks at how teams can have fun at work.

The value of humour

'Always remember – don't take yourself so seriously.'
Ben Zander, conductor and author

Humour overcomes tiredness. Energy is not only correlated to sleep but to participation and having fun participating. It is also a vital part of the triumph of the human spirit against impossible odds.

Fun is the opposite of what most people call professional – it is chaotic, it happens in the moment. It is also vital to have the ability to laugh at oneself and for a team to be able to laugh at their own efforts.

There are three key contributions that team members can make to creating fun at work.

Cheerfulness

Some days the last thing you might feel like being is cheerful. However, you could try faking it. When a colleague asks you how you're feeling, smile and say 'Wonderful, thank you!' rather than relating your woes. Acting this way can lead to genuine feelings of

Case study

One day a new product design team got together in a really off-the-wall mood and made fun of their product. The meeting was a great success and many new ideas were generated. The next week, everybody was in a serious mood and no new ideas were generated. The moral of this story is that there is a very close link between the 'Aha!' of invention and the 'haha' of humour.

31

Case study

A friend of mine, Jeremy, with whom I have run an endurance event, the 250-mile Western Isles Challenge, is always cheerful and laughing. I have never seen him miserable or upset. He can defuse any personal or team pressure by his sheer cheerfulness. He is an invaluable team member who brings much more to a team than his technical skills.

Where next?

Fish,
S Lundin; H Paul;
J Christensen,
Hodder &
Stoughton, 2000.

cheerfulness and can improve not only your mood but also that of your colleagues.

Play

Play is how we understand our world and build many personal relationships. It can involve team sports, reading clubs, attending a crafts workshop or a quiz night at the local pub. It allows us to be creative and take risks that too often seem to become impossible once we don a business suit. Generating play at work involves thinking about how tasks could be tackled from an unexpected point of view. For example:

- create an 'ideas zone' and provide lots of coloured pens, paper and craft materials – encourage others to use it as much as possible
- use creative thinking techniques, even in straightforward business meetings – for example, by using the storyboard technique for budget forecasts, or brainstorming ideas for a fundraising dinner
- invite a juggler or a musician into a team meeting and get them to teach the whole team to juggle or play an instrument.

Make someone's day

Here are some ways you can do this.

- Take in a cake that you have baked for the team.
- Buy someone a small present to say thank you and present it to them in front of the team.
- Offer to help a teammate who is struggling.
- Handwrite someone a personal note.
- Take the team tenpin bowling after work.

Go on, make someone smile – make their day.